At Issue

| Polygamy

Other Books in the At Issue Series:

At Issue

| Polygamy

Stefan Kiesbye, Book Editor

GREENHAVEN PRESS
A part of Gale, Cengage Learning

Detroit • New York • San Francisco • New Haven, Conn • Waterville, Maine • London

Elizabeth Des Chenes, *Director, Publishing Solutions*

© 2013 Greenhaven Press, a part of Gale, Cengage Learning

Gale and Greenhaven Press are registered trademarks used herein under license.

For more information, contact:
Greenhaven Press
27500 Drake Rd.
Farmington Hills, MI 48331-3535
Or you can visit our Internet site at gale.cengage.com

For product information and technology assistance, contact us at

Gale Customer Support, 1-800-877-4253
For permission to use material from this text or product, submit all requests online at
www.cengage.com/permissions

Further permissions questions can be emailed to permissionrequest@cengage.com

Articles in Greenhaven Press anthologies are often edited for length to meet page requirements. In addition, original titles of these works are changed to clearly present the main thesis and to explicitly indicate the author's opinion. Every effort is made to ensure that Greenhaven Press accurately reflects the original intent of the authors. Every effort has been made to trace the owners of copyrighted material.

Cover image © Images.com/Corbis.

LIBRARY OF CONGRESS CATALOGING-IN-PUBLICATION DATA

Polygamy / Stefan Kiesbye, book editor.
   p. cm. -- (At issue)
   Includes bibliographical references and index.
   ISBN 978-0-7377-6193-1 (hardcover) -- ISBN 978-0-7377-6194-8 (pbk.)
   1. Polygamy. 2. Polygamy--Religious aspects. 3. Polygamy--Law and legislation. I.
Kiesbye, Stefan.
   HQ981.P647 2012
   306.84'23--dc23

                                         2012023326

Printed in the United States of America
1 2 3 4 5 6 7 16 15 14 13 12

Contents

Introduction

The question of whether polygamy is an abomination or a viable alternative lifestyle has recently resurfaced in the media. New offerings from scripted and reality television, coupled with high-profile criminal cases, have stoked the interest of the public. The debate surrounding the issue is heated and ideologically charged. For many people, it's a question of personal freedom, while for others it is an issue of morals, of right and wrong.

Often overlooked in the polygamy debate is the fact that many men and women in monogamous relationships cheat on their partners, sometimes over long periods of time, thereby creating multiple, lasting bonds. Research published in the *Journal of Couple and Relationship Therapy* found that 50 percent of women and 60 percent of men will cheat during their marriage. Yet while women are traditionally seen as victims in a polygamous relationship—as well as victims of extramarital affairs—evolutionary psychologist Satoshi Kanazawa, in an October 4, 2009, article in *Psychology Today*, points out that "mating among all mammalian species (including humans) is a female choice; it happens whenever and with whomever the female wants, not whenever and with whomever the male wants."

As author Charles Orlando found out, dating websites have acknowledged that both men and women seek partners outside of marriage. Furthermore, "affairs are big business. Numerous websites are dedicated to connecting those looking to engage in . . . [extramarital intimate relationships]. Affairs Club.com, MarriedCafe.com, LonelyWivesAffairs.com are but the tip of the iceberg, and all have women and men signing up in droves," he writes in his April 14, 2011, article for Your Tango.com. He observes that "there isn't one 'type' of woman looking to cheat. . . . Some were looking to have sex, period.

Others were looking to subsidize their current relationship with a human connection . . . and if it led to sex, even better. But all were clear that they were not leaving their current relationship." In other words, they were looking to fulfill their physical and emotional needs with more than one partner.

In addition to adultery, serial monogamy—the skipping from one spouse to the next—also is the prerogative of both men and women, finds Natalie Angier, in a *New York Times* article from August 31, 2009. She contradicts the common wisdom that it is only men who use serial monogamy as "a socially sanctioned version of harem-building . . . like the sultan who hoards the local maidenry in a single convenient location, simply seeking to 'maximize his reproductive fitness.'" Relying on a study by researcher Monique Borgerhoff Mulder, Angier presents evidence that "at least in some non-Western cultures where conditions are harsh and mothers must fight to keep their children alive, serial monogamy is by no means a man's game, finessed by him and foisted on her. To the contrary . . . among the Pimbwe people of Tanzania . . . serial monogamy looks less like polygyny [the practice of one man marrying several women] than like a strategic beast that some evolutionary psychologists dismiss as quasi-fantastical: polyandry, one woman making the most of multiple mates."

"We're so wedded to the model that men will benefit from multiple marriages and women won't, that women are victims of the game," Dr. Borgerhoff Mulder is quoted. "But what my data suggest is that Pimbwe women are strategically choosing men, abandoning men and remarrying men as their economic situation goes up and down. . . . You can construe sequential relationships as being driven by male choice, in which case you'd call it polygyny, or by female choice, in which case you'd call it polyandry, but the capacity of women across cultures to dissolve relationships that aren't working has been much underestimated."

At Issue: Polygamy explores numerous debates regarding the practice of plural marriage—including spousal abuse, child abuse, legal and religious issues, and the possibility of finding love and meaning beyond traditional unions—in a time when conventional notions of marriage are being challenged.

1

Polygamy Persists Despite Opposition

AP Online

The Associated Press is an American news agency.

In the following viewpoint, former polygamist and historian Ben Bistline explains that despite outside opposition, polygamy will continue. Bistline has seen many polygamists jailed for their beliefs and contends that they believe it is necessary to gain their highest exaltation to heaven. These men and women have been taught polygamy since the day they were born, so Bistline argues it will never change, even with opposition and the arrest of others. Bistline believes that those arrested and prosecuted for polygamy only serve as martyrs and will not change the practice.

COLORADO CITY, Ariz.—Ben Bistline chuckles when asked to explain why the practice of polygamy persists. The outside world, he says, just doesn't get it.

"We just grew up in polygamy," said Bistline, a 70-something former polygamist and local historian. "It's part of our life. I don't know how else to say it."

Bistline has lived along the Utah-Arizona border since the neighboring towns of Colorado City, Ariz., and Hildale, Utah—home of the Fundamentalist Church of Jesus Christ of Latter Day Saints—were still known as Short Creek. He was there when Arizona authorities raided the community in 1953 in an attempt to stop plural marriages and has seen dozens of men and women jailed for their beliefs.

"They believe that it's necessary to gain their exaltation to the highest level of heaven," said Bistline, a resident of Cane Beds, which is just east of Colorado City. "They've been taught that since the day they were born. It won't change."

"Anybody who expects polygamy to go away is a fool."

Not even with the prosecution of FLDS leader Warren Jeffs.

"He's not the sole supporter of polygamy," said Lori Chatwin, a Colorado City woman who grew up there and married at 17. "It's a religious belief."

Jeffs, 50, was arrested Monday near Las Vegas after more than a year on the run. He appeared before a Nevada judge Thursday and said he will not fight extradition to Utah to face charges of rape by accomplice.

"Anybody who expects polygamy to go away is a fool. It's been here 100 years and is not going to go away because one guy gets arrested," said Flora Jessop, a former FLDS member who fled the community in 1996 and now works to help women and children who also want to leave the lifestyle.

The FLDS church is just one of a handful of Utah-based fundamentalist groups that continue to practice polygamy. Once a tenet of the early Church of Jesus Christ of Latter-day Saints, the practice was abandoned in 1890 as a condition of Utah's statehood.

The church now excommunicates any member found practicing polygamy and disavows the idea of "Mormon fundamentalists," although most Utah polygamists identify themselves that way.

If history is any indicator, Jeffs' legal troubles should only serve to move him toward martyrdom, said Ken Driggs, an Atlanta defense attorney who has written extensively about the legal history of polygamy.

"Historically, it's generally made martyrs out of the people who get prosecuted," he said. "They come back revered."

Jeffs is already revered as a prophet. As head of the church since 2002, he has controlled the sect's marriages, deciding whom and when women marry. He has performed most of the marriage ceremonies himself. He is known to demand obedience and has reportedly used even minor infractions as grounds for booting some men from the church, forcing them to leave their families behind.

More than any FLDS leader before him, Jeffs has used fear to manage his flock, Bistline said. But it's unfair to say that everyone lives and worships here under duress, he said.

"The majority don't want to leave," he said. "They're an intelligent people and within their belief of polygamy, they are a moral people."

Jessop doesn't deny that some in the FLDS community don't want to leave, but she also believes many are naive and lack experience to structure their lives and families another way.

What outsiders fail to understand is how deeply the practice is rooted in religious commitment and heritage, said Driggs.

"When you're taught from birth that if you don't live this way you're damned to hell for eternity, that's not a choice," she said.

Driggs said Jeffs' incarceration now and after any conviction would likely be seen by church members as another test of faith, but it might have a moderating effect on practices like underage marriages.

"That's where the legal pressure is coming from. It may not stop, it may just happen a lot less," he said. "But it won't stop plural marriage."

What outsiders fail to understand is how deeply the practice is rooted in religious commitment and heritage, said Driggs.

"It's been my experience down there that the women are as committed as the men, sometimes more so," he said. "(Outsiders) think it's about sex and power and domination, but it's about a lot of other things. This is what they were raised in and it's multigenerational. It's their culture."

2

Polygamy Is Detrimental to Marriage, Faith, and Society

Fay Voshell

Fay Voshell is a cum laude graduate of the University of Delaware and received her Master of Divinity from Princeton Theological Seminary, which awarded her the seminary's Charles Hodge Prize for Excellence in Systematic Theology. She was selected as one of the Delaware Republican party's "Winning Women" of 2008.

Film and television recently have begun to portray polygamous marriages in a positive light. Furthermore, some left-wing liberals assert that so-called plural marriages should be accepted as part of a broader definition of marriage. Yet America's newfound tolerance of fundamentalist Mormons and their families is dangerous—polygamy has the potential to negate women's rights and to render marriage and love meaningless. Regardless of assertions that such marriages are consensual, polygamy enslaves women and makes female children vulnerable to molestation and rape. Instead of favorably portraying a polygamist lifestyle, Hollywood should depict the negative consequences of allowing men to marry multiple wives.

Tinseltown is seeking to mainstream polygamous relationships.

Having long ago forsaken the favorable depiction of monogamy characterized by such shows as the long-running *Ad-*

Fay Voshell, "Kody Brown, His 'Sister Wives,' and the Return of Polygamy," *American Thinker*, September 2011. www.americanthinker.com. Copyright © 2011 by American Thinker. All rights reserved. Reproduced by permission.

ventures of Ozzie and Harriet (1952–1966) and *Father Knows Best* (1954–1960), Hollywood producers are outdoing themselves in portraying polygamy as just another lifestyle that should be accepted by Americans.

HBO's fictional series entitled *Big Love* was one of the shows which began the polygamy love affair among Hollywood producers. The show was followed by the reality series *Sister Wives*, starring the perennially grinning Kody Brown. Brown is legally married to one wife, but "spiritually" wed to three other spouses who live pseudo-harmoniously as one big, happy family with sixteen children. He is the latest calendar pinup for the sexually liberated left, which seems hell-bent on redefining marriage to the point of eliminating it altogether.

The real polygamous Brown family, having replaced TV's fictionalized *Big Love* family as the poster-family for polygamy, are now suing to make their choices legally legitimate, seeking to decriminalize "consensual" polygamous relationships— ironically, in Utah, of all places.

For those unfamiliar with the history of Utah, the state has been a stronghold of the Mormon faith since Brigham Young traveled to the American West in order to continue his and his followers' belief in polygamous practices without interference from the law. Young was husband to 55 wives. . . . He sired 57 children.

An Expression of Faith

The Mormon Church repudiated the actual practice of polygamy and wife-sharing in 1890 in order to join the Union. Though most Mormons are monogamous, outlying fundamentalist, polygamous Mormon sects still flourish in Utah and other states. Mr. Brown is one of the Mormon fundamentalists who justify the taking of multiple wives as an expression of faith.

Brown's lawyer, Jonathan Turley, has defended Brown's polygamous household in an article from the *New York Times* entitled "One Big, Happy Polygamous Family."

Mr. Turley writes that there are many polygamists in the U.S., among them fundamentalist Mormons and Muslims. It seems both groups are finding government intrusion into their personal lives insufferable.

Turley believes that just because Mr. Brown's family does not look like those of other Utah families, it doesn't mean they are criminals; rather, it simply means that "[p]olygamy is just one form among the many types of plural relationships in our society[.] . . . Homosexuals and polygamists do have a common interest: the right to be left alone as consenting adults." The Browns, he continues, "want to be allowed to create a loving family according to the values of their faith."

There are red-light indicators that Mr. Turley's arguments in defense of Kody Brown's polygamous family are being taken quite seriously.

The Possibility of Legalizing Polygamy

For instance, according to a recent survey taken of Canadian Mormons, fully half would like to see the re-institutionalization of multiple marriages as a holy practice of their faith.

Second, as noted by Nina Bernstein in her *New York Times* article entitled "In Secret, Polygamy Follows Africans to New York," the influx of Muslim immigrants into New York City [NYC] (and elsewhere) has meant that many have brought their polygamous practices with them. She writes that most of the women in polygamous households, of which there are thousands in NYC alone, have spoken bitterly of polygamy.

> They said their participation was dictated by an African culture of female subjugation and linked polygamy to female genital cutting and domestic violence. That view is echoed

by most research on plural marriages, including studies of West African immigrants in France, where the government estimates that 120,000 people live in 20,000 polygamous families.

But in a milieu such as NYC, imbued as it is with multiculturalism and a "don't ask, don't tell" mentality concerning sexual mores, no one is paying much attention to the establishment of polygamous households. Further, Bernstein ominously notes, "[I]f the household breaks up, the wives' legal status is murky at best, with little case law to guide decisions on marital property or benefits."

The push for gay marriage was based on the monogamous principle, which was used as a model for allowing same-sex unions. But whatever the motives and longings of those espousing gay marriage, as Justice Antonin Scalia memorably noted in his dissent in *Lawrence v. Texas* (which struck down anti-sodomy laws), the decision would mean a sexual free-for-all, opening the door for the legalization of "bigamy, same-sex marriage, adult incest, prostitution, masturbation, adultery, fornication, bestiality and obscenity."

Multiplicity of partners automatically ensures unequal treatment before the law, whether it is "consensual" or not.

The Consequences of Polygamy

While the left may sneer at Justice Scalia's list of predictions, it is fair to ask just what the consequences of the establishment and legalization of polygamy in the West would be. For rest assured: the practice would not long remain an exotic and titillating source for TV reality shows, but would multiply quickly, bringing many woes with it.

First, legal polygamy would guarantee that women in the West in polygamous relationships would begin to resemble third-world women in multiple marriages. The achievements of the struggle for women's rights in Europe, the Americas, and indeed around the world would be blown to smithereens, for the premise of equal rights for men and women begins with the equality monogamous marriage provides as a bedrock for equal rights for men and women before the law.

Monogamous marriages have never been and never will be perfect; however, for all the vicissitudes [difficulties] and inequities associated with monogamous marriage over the centuries, the truth of the matter is that monogamy has been the foremost reason for the elevation of women to equality with men. The one-on-one relationship ratifies equality in social conduct and before the law. Polygamy destroys the hope of equality at the core level, making the relationship between the man and the women inherently unequal, to copy a phrase from *Plessy v. Ferguson*. As in the case of *Dred Scott v. Sanford*, it automatically consigns human beings—in this case, women—to a status less than men and thus not as fully human as men.

Multiplicity of partners automatically ensures unequal treatment before the law, whether it is "consensual" or not. The first duty of the law is that another person not be permitted to do harm. Polygamy automatically does harm to the woman, even when she consents to be one of multiple spouses.

Polygamy Degrades Women

The fact of the matter is that the destruction of monogamous marriage and the institutionalization of polygamy will automatically result in the reduction of women to mere concubines, with all the evils attendant to that lesser status. Historically, wherever polygamy has reigned, women and children suffer, and male dominance, in the real sense of that often overused and misapplied term, is guaranteed. Male dominance means sexual dominance, among other things. The woman is reduced to a plaything, her capacities as a being equal to man subsumed under the male. Her influence and significance are divided among a plurality of wives and concubines—a fate scarcely contemplated by sentimental theorists who go on about "consenting adults."

One need only read the stories of polygamous relationships in the Old Testament, written thousands of years ago, to see clearly the absolute misery the practice caused for all involved—a reason Christ called for marriage to reflect the initial created order of Adam and Eve. The exhortations of the Hebrew prophets to honor the wife of one's youth plus Christ's articulation of the monogamous principle have been a bedrock on which women's rights have been forwarded.

The misery of women mired in polygamous relationships is stunningly depicted in the brilliant film *Raise the Red Lantern* (1991), starring Gong Li. Director Yimou Zhang avoids idealization of concubinage and polygamy, preferring the cold eye of realism. He depicts the vicious rivalry among the wives, the betrayals leading to the death of rivals, the dismissal and denigration of the aging concubines, and the downward trend toward pedophilia as younger and younger women are desired. His unrelenting cinematic eye focuses on the utter sexual and economic captivity of the wives and is the perfect riposte to current liberal dementia concerning polygamy.

Sexual Slaves

But one does not need to read Old-Testament stories or view Zhang's film to understand that women are basically little more than sexual slaves when polygamy is a societal practice. The point is reinforced time and again by societies dominated by religions allowing polygamy. Attendant to the misery and subjection of women is the unequal treatment concerning their children, who are also completely under the dominance of fathers.

Just as pertinent, in our own country, the glamorization and defense of polygamy typical of liberal defense lawyer Turley has been shown for what it really is—a dangerous fiction.

Polygamy kills the romantic idea that somewhere there is a man or woman who completes a relationship.

The ugly reality was exposed during the recent, notorious trial of Warren Jeffs, who is the head of the Utah-based Mormon Fundamentalist LDS [Latter-Day Saints] Church. Jeffs' sect believes that polygamy brings exaltation in heaven. Cynics believe that Jeffs found exaltation of quite another variety by sexually abusing underage girls. The prosecutors exposed polygamy's horrors before a traumatized jury, playing a tape in which Jeffs had recorded himself—before onlookers—raping a twelve-year-old "spiritual bride." Jeffs is but one example of aging men who choose younger and younger "brides" to add to their harems.

Regardless of the exposure of the realities of polygamy and the disgust with which the jury reacted to Jeffs' prurient sexual practices, liberals continue to push for polygamy as just an "alternate lifestyle" without fully comprehending the deleterious, indeed catastrophic consequences to society.

The End of Romance

It is to be doubted that the left has contemplated, for instance, that polygamy would mean the death of the Western concept of romance. The Platonic ideal of the other half and the Christian ideal of monogamy have informed romantic literature for centuries. Polygamy kills the romantic idea that somewhere there is a man or woman who completes a relationship. Ironically, romance between one woman and one man is a subject Hollywood delights in portraying time and again, following one of the unconscious and subliminal foundations of Western society. Polygamy destroys romance.

To paraphrase a quote from Mustapha Mond, leader of the radical new sexual order in Aldous Huxley's prescient *Brave New World*, written in 1933:

> He waved his hand; and it was as though, with an invisible feather whisk, he had brushed away a little dust, and the dust was Orpheus and Eurydice; some spider webs, Tristan and Isolde, Romeo and Juliet. Whisk. Whisk—and where was Dante and Beatrice, Abelard and Heloise? Whisk—and those specks of antique legends, Lancelot and Guinevere? Whisk, the other half; whisk, eternal fidelity. Whisk. Whisk, whisk.

The idea of faithfulness as a virtue would vanish overnight were polygamy to become a law of the land.

We are told by liberals and "moderate" Republicans time and time again that social issues should take a backseat to economic issues. The fact of the matter is that the two are inextricably intertwined. Wherever polygamy is encouraged and wherever it becomes dominant, there will be poverty—economic, political, and spiritual.

The basic principle of monogamous marriage between one man and one woman constitutes one of the moral foundations on which the entire societal edifice rests. Along with the principle of the right to life, the principle of monogamous marriage demands the support and protection of not just the Church universal, but also the state.

Fighting for Monogamous Marriage

The solution to the present confusion over the issue of marriage lies with those committed to the Judeo-Christian principle of monogamous marriage. Since the mainline churches and liberal Jewish synagogues are rapidly capitulating to the demands of gay marriage activists—most recently the Presbyterian Church USA—evangelicals and Catholics must fight for

[the] monogamous principle that has characterized the West for hundreds of years. Both should and must unite to stand up for the monogamous marriage covenant, lobbying with an intensity that matches or excels the mad obsession of those radicals who seek to overturn one of the foundational mores of Western civilization.

Those who believe in sexual faithfulness between partners should also join the fight. Faithfulness to one's partner is one of the last remaining vestiges of the principle of monogamy. It is still honored, at least as a virtue to aspire to, among gay rights activists and some other liberals. The idea of faithfulness as a virtue would vanish overnight were polygamy to become a law of the land.

The West would be racing even faster toward a sexual free-for-all, a world in which "everyone belongs to everyone else," as Huxley notes.

There would come a time, as Mustapha Mond reminds his eager students, when the very concept of monogamy would appear hopelessly antiquated. Why, he says, can you believe that at one time, people had different ideas? Can you imagine that at one time not everyone belonged to everyone else?

If a coalition of those who oppose polygamy is not gathered, and if the fight for the monogamous principle is not enjoined, the rapid installation of polygamy in the West, with the inevitable ills attendant to it—among the worst being a catastrophic setback of women's and children's rights—will continue apace.

3

Polygamy Poses Challenges to Men and Women Alike

Natalie O'Brien

Natalie O'Brien is an Australian journalist and has worked for such publications as The Australian *and the* Sydney Sun-Herald, *as well as for Big Splash Media.*

Australia and Great Britain prohibit polygamy but recognize polygamous marriages that have been legally recognized overseas. These laws, combined with new media interest in so-called alternative lifestyles, have reopened the debate about polygamy and its consequences for society. Lost in the hype and the sensationalist coverage are the serious challenges that men and women in polygamous families face everyday. In such families, the women, or "sister-wives," often are not treated equally by their husband and supporting multiple families can put serious strains on men's time and health.

It seemed the natural thing to do for Trad, 44, who lives in Sydney's western suburbs.

Trad had already lived through the experience of being the son of his father's second wife, who became part of the family after the first wife became too ill to look after their children. A childhood spent living with a mother and a stepmother was completely normal. "There was nothing out of the ordinary," Trad tells *The Australian*. "My mother and my stepmother were always best friends. They never argued. She looked at my mum like she was her sister."

Their extended family took shape in the northern Lebanese city of Tripoli in the 1960s. "That society was very openminded," Trad recalls. "Even though it was not the norm. I was not aware of any other family with that sort of relationship. But generally, I found people didn't care as long as the relationship was a peaceful one."

But Trad's mother warned him not to talk about the family arrangements, saying people really were not that openminded.

The Issue of Social Stigma

Whether a second wife would work in the Trad household remains another issue. The Trads say they have discussed the idea only in principle. Trad's wife, Hanifeh, is not against the idea of having another woman in her husband's life. She says she has enough confidence in herself not to let it affect her ego. However, she's concerned of the effect it might have on her children and how they would be affected by the stigma.

While it remains illegal for a married man to marry another woman in Britain, polygamous marriages that take place in countries where the arrangement is legal will be legally recognised.

"We don't know whether it would work for us. We have only intellectualised, we have never practised it," Trad says.

The family has been subjected to a barrage of criticism after Trad went against his mother's advice and commented publicly on polygamy this week. Trad supports a call by imam Sheik Khalil Chami, from the Islamic Welfare Centre in Lakemba, NSW [New South Wales], for polygamous marriages to be legally recognised.

It follows the British Government's announcement in February [2008] of new guidelines that legally recognise polygamous marriages and allow men to claim social welfare for each spouse. While it remains illegal for a married man to marry another woman in Britain, polygamous marriages that take place in countries where the arrangement is legal will be legally recognised. The move came a year after the British Government admitted polygamous marriages were flourishing in Britain and that nearly 1000 men were living legally with multiple wives.

Polygamy and the Law

There are no official figures showing how many people live in polygamous relationships in Australia. But Chami says he's asked almost weekly to perform polygamous religious ceremonies.

Chami has refused, but he and Trad agree that officially recognising polygamous marriages would help protect the rights of the women in these relationships.

Trad says women are left in a vulnerable financial position if the man dies. "If this woman has wilfully chosen to enter into this relationship and make a lifelong commitment to this person to be married, it shouldn't matter," he says.

"If it was a business and the business had four partners, we'd recognise that, but why don't we recognise it when it comes to consensual relationships among adults?"

Under Islamic or sharia law, multiple wives and children must be treated equally.

In Australia it is illegal to enter into a polygamous marriage. But the federal government, like Britain, recognises relationships that have been legally recognised overseas, including polygamous marriages. This allows second wives and children to claim welfare and benefits.

But anyone like Trad considering a polygamous marriage within Australia has been warned off by federal Attorney-General Robert McClelland.

"Everyone should be on notice that the law in Australia is that marriage is between a man and a woman to the exclusion of all others," McClelland says. "It's based on the culture of our community and polygamous relationships are entirely inconsistent with that culture and indeed with the law."

Under Islamic or sharia law, multiple wives and children must be treated equally. If the father dies, then wives and children equally share his estate.

Polygamy Faces a New Reality

Australian Federation of Islamic Councils interim president Haset Sali says the Koran makes it clear the Islamic legal system can provide for more than one wife.

But that was written when many women suffered in unfortunate financial circumstances and the ratio of women to men was about three to one. Sali says the Koran also states the overriding principal that the man must be fair to each wife and treat them equally. "I don't know anyone who can be 100 per cent fair to both women," Sali says. "It might have been appropriate in ancient history, but I don't see it as something that works in the 21st century."

Polygamy is common in Indonesia, where most of the population is Muslim, but it remains a controversial lifestyle choice. A popular view in Indonesia is that polygamy can be an easy way out of an unhappy marriage or a means for a restless husband to satisfy wandering desires without the bother and financial penalty of divorce.

However, late last year the Indonesian courts upheld the right of a man to take another wife after a Jakarta businessman took his case to court. Despite his victory, Mohommad Insa was disappointed at limitations put on the practice, including the requirement that an existing spouse be informed of her husband's intention.

"In Islam there is no such regulation, such as needing the agreement of your wife, or that you can only do it if she's crippled," an indignant Insa said.

In the US, polygamy sects and practising polygamists have continual run-ins with the law. The Fundamentalist Church of Jesus Christ of Latter-Day Saints is the best known of the various polygamist sects surviving in North America. It has been targeted by authorities since 2002, when one member, Tom Green, 37, was convicted of child rape. Green, who lived with five wives and 29 children in a Utah trailer camp, had impregnated his 13-year-old "spiritual wife".

Although the practice of polygamy was brought to Utah by the Mormons in 1847, the church outlawed taking multiple wives in 1890, whereupon some sects broke away, believing polygamy paves the way to heaven.

Although polygamy has been practised in clannish compounds since, Green's conviction was the first in a half century.

The leader of the Fundamentalist Church of Jesus Christ of Latter-Day Saints [FLDS], Warren Jeffs, 51, was found guilty of rape charges in September last year [2007], stemming from the marriage of a girl, 14, against her will to a cousin. Jeffs was convicted on two charges of acting as an accomplice to rape.

Jeffs, a self-proclaimed prophet whose followers believe he is descended from Jesus Christ, was arrested in August 2006 outside Las Vegas after being included on the FBI's [Federal Bureau of Investigation] 10 Most Wanted list.

"Women are vessels to be worn out in childbirth and girls are having children at age 14, 15, 16."

Polygamy Might Lead to Sexual Abuse

In April [2008], US authorities removed 468 children from a polygamist sect at the ranch of the Fundamentalist Church of Jesus Christ of Latter-Day Saints near Eldorado, Texas, amid allegations of systemic sexual and physical abuse. A search was conducted after a girl, 16, called a local family violence shelter to report her husband, 50, had beaten and raped her.

Officials alleged the sect's girls were being groomed to have sex with middle-aged "spiritual husbands" as soon as they reached puberty and boys were indoctrinated to continue the cycle of abuse. However, in May the Texas Supreme Court ruled the removal of the children was unwarranted because they were not in immediate danger.

Former Utah journalist Andrea Moore-Emmett says there are 13 groups practising polygamy, which has been abandoned by the mainstream Mormon Church. Moore-Emmett says she fled Utah after publishing a book, *God's Brothel*, which detailed the abuse of women and children in fundamentalist communities. "Women are vessels to be worn out in childbirth and girls are having children at age 14, 15, 16," she has said.

Polygamy has even been embraced by popular culture, with leading US cable channel HBO producing a television drama series called *Big Love*, about a Viagra-popping polygamist and his three wives and families living in suburban America. The series, which screens in Australia on SBS, has upset many Mormons who claim it reinforces old stereotypes about the religion, which banned polygamy more than 100 years ago.

The central theme of *Big Love* revolves around the husband's attempts to deal with the conflicts, jealousy and financial strain that come with having three families living in three adjoining houses with a common back yard. Former polygamists are concerned the series trivialises the real problems polygamous families face.

Polygamy Needs to Be Discussed Openly and Fairly

Silma Ihram, an Anglo-Australian convert to Islam and one of the pioneers of Muslim education in Australia, believes it is time the issue of multiple partners is debated in Australia. Ihram says it is not just a Muslim issue. "Take away the Islamic tag because that is irrelevant," she says. "There are many people whose marriages are not registered and there are a large number of people having affairs." She says there are very few people who have polygamous marriages and believes most women are smart, educated, financially independent and don't want it.

Still, she believes the issue should be talked about openly. "Where are we going with the family structure? Where are we going on relationships? We need to ask the questions: How important is it to have a one-on-one relationship and is it acceptable to have more than partner?"

Trad says he talks about polygamy to help people appreciate the importance of protecting their marriage. "I talk about personal experiences when I came close to considering a second relationship to show people that we can all get through these thoughts and inclinations and that what is important is holding on to and saving our existing marriages, which should take priority over all other emotions," he says.

A successful Lebanese businessman in Tripoli, who does not wish to be named, says he was mindful of preserving his first marriage when he entered his second. The 30-year-old had married his childhood sweetheart and had several children when he fell in love with his second wife.

He said wanted to keep his first wife happy and not to penalise her in any way because she had done him no wrong. But taking the second wife proved expensive, exhausting and potentially fatal.

He now runs two businesses and works long hours to pay for the flats, cars and clothes both families require.

It leaves him little energy to provide equal time and love for two wives.

He is now dealing with the aftermath of a fire bomb attack on the apartment of his second wife, perpetrated, he suspects, by his extremely jealous first wife.

4

Polygamous Communities Often Limit Women's Rights

Jessica Mack

Jessica Mack is a global women's rights advocate. Her writings can be found at Gender Across Borders, RH Reality Check, Alter-Net, Feministe, and other websites.

While having multiple spouses is in itself not problematic, polygamous communities often display a disregard for women's rights. These communities are often isolated from the outside world, and in many cases they foster misogynist behavior. It is hypocritical, however, to condemn polygamist communities such as the Fundamentalist Church of Jesus Christ of Latter-Day Saints, and to overlook the discrimination women still face in the larger society. Oppression exists everywhere, and the discussion about gender equality should not stop at polygamy.

The British Columbia Supreme Court is currently undertaking a fascinating and controversial review of Canada's polygamy law, which has outlawed the practice since the 1890's. The law is under review for possible violation of religious rights guaranteed under the Canadian constitution.

Polygamy—whereby an individual (man or woman) has more than one spouse—has long been a divisive issue, not least because it is considered bad for women, sometimes leading to early and forced marriage, incest, pedophilia and other abuses.

Polygamy Is Not Necessarily Unfair to Women

Although the practice is widespread across cultures, we know it best in North America as characterized by the Fundamentalist Church of Jesus Christ of Latter-Day Saints (FLDS), a Mormon offshoot. In 2008, more than 500 women and children were removed forcibly from the FLDS Yearning For Zion ranch in Texas over suspected abuse. Characterized by images of women with ubiquitous French braids, drab-colored dresses and scads of children in tow, such large FLDS communities have come to epitomize polygamy, with residents living cloistered from, and oftentimes outside the legal jurisdiction of, the rest of society.

But is polygamy *inherently* bad for women?

The practice of taking numerous spouses, in and of itself, doesn't seem to be the root cause of the problem. After all, there are clear examples of polyandry (in which one woman has several husbands, as opposed to polygyny, with one man and several women), but abuse and oppression of men in these cases rarely, if ever, comes up.

Perhaps instead, the problem with polygamy (or, really, polygyny) is that the legal structure of marriage codifies an underlying discrimination against women. Reports from polygamous communities often point to early and forced marriage, in which the institution of marriage serves as both a shield for, and weapon of, sexist behavior.

Very often, it's religious minority practices that are especially flagged as being harmful. Religious majorities don't tend to come under the same scrutiny.

Also, polygamy is often practiced secretively and in cloistered religious communities that exist quite literally outside the norms of broader society. This situation can create impunity for those men who are abusing women.

The Issue of Polygamy Needs to Be Discussed Without Prejudice

The uneasy tension between religious freedom and the rights of women lies at the heart of the current case in Canada, which concerns two Mormon fundamentalist polygamist factions in Bountiful, British Columbia.

One of the more lucid points made so far in the trial was by religious studies professor Lori Beaman, who testified, "Don't look to stereotypes when deciding the fate of polygamy law." While polygamy has a grave track record when it comes to women's rights, we should at the same time be wary when people invoke the 'feminism card' when a practice happens to lie outside religious and cultural norms.

Beaman continues:

> Very often, it's religious minority practices that are especially flagged as being harmful. Religious majorities don't tend to come under the same scrutiny.

Agreed, but shouldn't we be looking more critically at religious minorities in addition to religious majorities? And, really, shouldn't we be looking at anyone who dares think they can limit the rights of women in this day and age?

Other Oppressive Practices Remain

While it's established that polygamy can be a source of oppression for women, to over-simplify the practice and construe it as *necessarily* generating abuse seems unproductive. Instead, by attending to the nuances of experience and relying on women's voices themselves—the Canadian hearing is including a range of dissonant testimonies—we might be more successful in both rooting out the causes of harm and raising tolerance for alternative lifestyles.

If we are going to pull out women's rights as the issue here, making the legality of polygamy about the unjust tolerance for women's rights abuses, let's *really* make it about that, across the board. Let's use polygamy as *one* example where oppression remains (albeit perhaps not unilaterally), and an entry point into honest discussions about the many others.

5

Polygamy Harms Marriage and Society

Rebekah Hebbert

Rebekah Hebbert is the managing editor at The Prince Arthur Herald. *She writes event blogs for political conferences, and she conducts research and writes policy briefs for a pro-life political party.*

Trying to decriminalize polygamy, the Fundamentalist Church of Jesus Christ of Latter-Day Saints (FLDS) and their community in Bountiful, British Columbia, have come under intense scrutiny. Stories of child abuse have surfaced but also tales of peaceful, communal living and harmony among families and "sister-wives." Even if polygamy does offer benefits to its practioners, the practice upsets society's most basic values. Polygamy challenges the cultural norms of Canadian society and harms children and the institution of marriage.

*O*h, *I would sing and dance with rejoicing if celestial [polygamous] marriage was no longer considered criminal. I believe in my religion and way of life. Our family could all take the same last name. We would be able to have the benefits of Canada as other Canadians have. We would use the money we spend on fighting for our religion to build nice housing for the families ... We would be able to live in peace.*

Rebekah Hebbert, "Polygamy: What Harm Does It Do?," *MercatorNet*, March 2011. www.mercatornet.com. Copyright © 2011 by Rebekah Hebbert. All rights reserved. Reproduced by permission.

That was Witness Four, speaking in the British Columbia (Canada) Supreme Court about the alleged religious rights of a breakaway Mormon sect to practice polygamy.

According to the FLDS (Fundamentalist Church of Jesus Christ of Latter-Day Saints) and others on the side of decriminalizing polygamy, Canada, the land of hope and freedom, is persecuting some of its most vulnerable citizens—men and women who choose to peacefully express a minority religion, who ask nothing more than to be left alone and not live in the daily fear of being jailed and harassed for their faith.

Is this possible? In a country that takes minority rights so seriously that entire institutions are dedicated to weeding out even the smallest hints of prejudice? What have we become?

She learned the identity of her much older husband thirty minutes before she married him as a just-turned-17-year-old, crossed the Canadian border under false pretences, and came to live with him and her other three "sister-wives".

Religious Freedom vs. Human Rights

But wait a minute, this religious minority is also accused of involvement in the trafficking and abuse of young teenaged girls, subjecting children to dysfunctional and abusive families, exploiting young men, trapping women in a world of pain, the flagrant and public breech of laws that would protect the most vulnerable. Is it possible that Canada has turned a blind eye to all of this?

And what will happen now that the judiciary has to decide which should prevail: freedom of religion, or some of the most basic values and norms of Canadian society?

The question pits Canada's anti-polygamy law, section 293 of the Criminal Code, against the Canadian Charter of Rights and Freedom guarantee to "freedom of conscience and religion"—in this case the freedom of a FLDS/Mormon offshoot community in Bountiful B.C. This community believes that "plural marriages" are necessary in order to reach the Celestial Kingdom. Opposing that claim is a collection of organizations who contend that the abuses of polygamy are so grievous, and the harm to individuals and societies so great, that the law is a justifiable infringement on religious and individual rights.

What kinds of harm? Allegations against FLDS members include the water torture of babies (holding children face up under a running tap if they cry when spanked), marriage of girls as young as 12 or 14 (statutory rape), sexual, mental, and physical abuse of children, immigration fraud, unfair treatment of young men (due to shortage of brides), forced/coerced marriage, and more.

Perhaps some of the most affecting testimony came from Witness Four, quoted above. She learned the identity of her much older husband thirty minutes before she married him as a just-turned-17-year-old, crossed the Canadian border under false pretences, and came to live with him and her other three "sister-wives". Six months later, with no prior notice or consultation with his other wives, her husband married a 15 year old girl, who enrolled in grade nine that year as a married woman. It never occurred to anyone involved that this might be in any way improper. No one called the authorities. The marriage must have been a revelation from God and, therefore, it was right.

Keeping in Mind the Rights of Children

Another tragic story is told by a woman who refused, as a 13 year old, to marry the prophet Rulon Jeffs, then in his 80s. For this she was sent to work for a Bountiful lumber business. Laboring in sub zero conditions without proper protective clothing, she was reminded again and again by the "authorities" that if she would just submit to an arranged marriage it could all end. Trapped, terrified, and abandoned by her family she finally gave way and agreed to get married, at the age of 17.

But is this kind of harm, or any harm, inherent in polygamy? Surely monogamy has its own problems?

Dr. Margaret Somerville, Samuel Gale Professor of Law at McGill University, in an interview with *MercatorNet* suggests that while not all alleged harms are inherent in polygamy, some indeed are.

"My primary objection would be for the children . . . I believe that family units are primarily for the benefit of the children. Of course they are for the benefit of the adults involved as well, but if there is a clash between what adults want and what children need I give priority to the children."

"Children are best off with their mother and father, preferably their own biological parents unless an exception is justified as being in the best interests of a particular child. . . . Polygamy is an alternative adult arrangement, which is also difficult for some of the children who become adults within that arrangement." (Note the abuses chronicled above.)

"If you say that marriage is simply a social or cultural construct, which is what same-sex marriage says it is, and it has nothing to do with giving a child his own biological parents, then you could say that we could design marriage however we like."

Others contend that the abuses chronicled in Bountiful by both supporters and detractors are best fought by the legalization of polygamy. Some point to the idyllic picture of peace, love, and cooperation painted by many of the polygamous women, and suggest that the needs of the vulnerable would rather be served by bringing polygamy into the open, where abuse could be reported by women no longer afraid of prosecution for polygamy, and where justice and freedom of religion could coexist peacefully.

Redefining Marriage

But does society have a larger interest in banning polygamy? If some of these abuses are inherent to polygamy, can even legalizing it help? What could this do to the moral fabric of our society?

Margaret Somerville again speaks of the danger of redefining marriage, particularly for children. She has contended for years that allowing same sex marriage (as has been done in Canada), would make it difficult to justify shutting the door on polygamy.

"If you say that marriage is simply a social or cultural construct, which is what same-sex marriage says it is, and it has nothing to do with giving a child his own biological parents, then you could say that we could design marriage however we like. It could be four men and three women, or whatever you want to have.

"What a monogamous relationship, one man and one woman, does is that it builds marriage around a biological reality. Actually, unlike same sex marriage, polygamy also builds marriage around a biological reality too but it doesn't do it equally between men and women.

"I think it's a matter of both biology and cultural values, and our western democratic societies' cultural values are most definitely [in favour of] one man and one woman, and polygamy threatens that just as same sex marriage threatened that. Polygamy threatens it on the monogamous level, same sex marriage threatened it on the biological level."

"Once you move away from that fundamental monogamous procreational relationship . . . you start designing marriage however you like it, whether it is same sex marriage, whether it is polygamy either in the form of polygyny (one man with many wives) or polyandry (one woman with many husbands)." Or, indeed, what some of the sexual avant garde are calling "polyamory".

The children and women of Bountiful tell stories of wrenching abuse, and peaceful contentment. The Supreme Court is given a simple but difficult and critical choice. To choose to restrict the religious practice of some in the interests of preserving the traditional values of Canadian culture, or to accede to another redefinition of marriage and accept the collateral damage of broken lives in the name of freedom.

6

Polygamy Is Harmful to Children's Development

Pete Vere

Canadian Pete Vere is a canonical consultant for a number of diocesan tribunals, a sessional professor of canon law with Catholic Distance University, a regular columnist with the Wanderer, *and a senior reporter with* The Interim, *a pro-life monthly newspaper. His work also appears frequently in* This Rock *magazine and* The Washington Times. *He is the co-author of* Surprised by Canon Law: 150 Questions Catholics Ask about Canon Law; Surprised by Canon Law 2: More Questions Catholics Ask about Canon Law; *and* More Catholic Than the Pope: An Inside Look at Extreme Traditionalism.

Former members of the Fundamentalist Church of Jesus Christ of Latter-Day Saints (FLDS) have asserted that many FLDS children are physically abused, and many teenage girls are forced into marriages with men not of their choosing. Growing up secluded and without any relatives outside their community, young FLDS members are afraid to leave or seek outside help. They have poor job skills and, should they decide to leave, end up living on the streets. Whether or not polygamy is a viable way of life, child abuse within FLDS compounds needs to be addressed.

Texas law enforcement authorities removed 416 children from a fundamentalist Mormon compound after receiving a phone call alleging sexual and physical abuse. While information has since surfaced to suggest that the phone call was a hoax, Texas child-protection services continue their investigation. The children are members of the Fundamentalist Church of Jesus Christ of Latter-Day Saints [FLDS].

The FLDS is one of the most well-known polygamous offshoots of the Mormon movement. Its leader, Warren Jeffs, has frequently been in the news over the past couple years, first when the FBI [Federal Bureau of Investigation] added him to its Ten Most Wanted list and secondly when a Utah state court convicted him of twice being an accomplice to rape.

The sect extends into Canada, where it runs a commune in Bountiful, B.C. [British Columbia]. Yet, the B.C. government fears following in the footsteps of its Texas counterpart. With the passage of Canada's same-sex "marriage" legislation, B.C. officials are concerned any action against the commune would lead to the courts declaring anti-polygamy laws unconstitutional.

Yet, as Texas courts decide whether to return the children or place them in foster care, several former FLDS members have stepped forward and said the sect's polygamous practices are harmful to women and children.

The FLDS forced Kathleen to marry her step-brother when she was a teenager.

A History of Abuse

Rena and Kathleen Mackert are sisters who were born into the FLDS. The women spoke to *The Interim* through Tapestry Against Polygamy (Polygamy.org), a Utah-based organization that helps adults and children leaving polygamous relationships.

Tapestry spokeswoman Roweena Erickson, a refugee from another polygamous sect, said the sisters' experience is common to that of women and children raised in polygamous organizations.

"I was severely beaten as a child," Rena said, "and my father sexually abused me from the time I was three-and-a-half years old." Kathleen recalls trying to commit suicide when she was six. "To me, as a six-year-old, I would rather end that life I was trapped in," she said. "I felt I was being raised as a slave in modern-day America."

The FLDS forced Kathleen to marry her step-brother when she was a teenager. The marriage only added to her emotional turmoil. "One day, he's your brother and the next day, he's your husband," she said. Additionally, she would break down emotionally whenever a man admired her beauty, because the compliment triggered memories of her father's words whenever he sexually molested her.

Rena was also forced to marry a step-brother as a teenager. The marriage was loveless, she said. Shortly before the couple's fifth wedding anniversary, Rena's husband abandoned polygamy, Rena and the couple's three children.

The FLDS then ordered Rena to marry another sister's husband. She refused. She was in her early 20s, while the man was close to 60. While being taken to task by the FLDS leader for her disobedience, she denounced her father for having sexually molested her as a child. The leader excommunicated her.

"They took my children away, placed them with my father and mother and told (the children) I had abandoned them," Rena said. The FLDS forbade any contact between Rena and her children. They would be whisked away whenever Rena tried to visit. Yet Rena's biggest concern was that her children were now under the care of her father, who had physically and sexually abused her as a child.

Polygamy Puts Women and Children at Risk

Rena's children were returned a year later after a chance encounter with an attorney at the restaurant where she worked.

Yet, Rena's plight is common to most vulnerable adults and children who are born into polygamous sects and then try to leave.

They have nobody to turn to, as they are not permitted to socialize outside of their sect. Additionally, poor education and few job skills limit employment opportunities in the real world. And because these polygamous groups operate secretively and little is known about the particulars of their inner workings, finding a qualified therapist is difficult.

> *Often referred to as the "lost boys of polygamy," many polygamous sects excommunicate large numbers of their teenage boys for the most trivial infractions.*

The children seized in Texas will need a lot of support, Rena said. "Most believe they're condemned to hell. Many will end up alcoholics, drug addicts, strippers, prostitutes, criminals and prisoners." Polygamy has this effect on teenagers, because girls are seen mainly as sex objects, while boys are seen by older men as competition for the girls.

Often referred to as the "lost boys of polygamy," many polygamous sects excommunicate large numbers of their teenage boys for the most trivial infractions. Once excommunicated, the boys are left on the street without any financial or emotional support. The girls are then given as wives to men as old as 70 years of age.

Leaving Polygamous Communities Can Be Traumatic

"Many of the lost boys have been sexually molested and don't know how to relate to other people," Rena said. "Many commit suicide." This raises another difficulty faced by Rena, Kathleen and others who have escaped polygamy: the lack of a father figure while growing up makes it difficult to identify with a father.

Both Rena and Kathleen hope that in the debate over polygamy and its effects upon women and children, the state of Texas will not allow [itself] . . . to be drawn into a debate over religion.

"This has nothing to do with faith," Kathleen said. "This is about children being abused."

7

Polygamy Is Not Necessarily Harmful to Children's Development

Lee Kinkade

Lee Kinkade writes for Slate *and other publications and lives in Virginia, where she grew up in a commune.*

When stories of Fundamentalist Mormon groups are in the news, people should refrain from jumping to conclusions and condemning alternative lifestyles. Experiments with open, polyamorous families and life in communes have always existed, and children growing up inside these communities can have normal lives—even if their "normal" is different from that of mainstream America. The portrayal in the media of Mormon polygamists has been crude and often devoid of sympathy for customs and rituals varying from the norm. However, children growing up with several mothers, fathers, and with many step-siblings are not necessarily suffering from the lifestyle their biological parents chose. Many are cared for, nurtured, and educated.

Over the next few days [in June 2008], the state of Texas will continue returning more than 450 children removed from a polygamous Mormon ranch to their families. According to the ruling of the 3rd Circuit Court of Appeals, the state did not prove that the children were in immediate danger. "Without such proof," 38 mothers of the children argued, "the district court was required to return the children to their parents and abused its discretion by failing to do so." The Texas Supreme Court agreed.

The children who were removed and the parents to whom they are returned seem like strangers from a distant world (or time) to you. But not to me. When I listen to the media describing their lives, they feel like distant kin. As the story unfolded, I found that I had more in common with these children than with people bringing me news of them.

Growing Up in a Commune

I grew up in an intentional community—that's *commune* to you. My childhood was as far from fundamentalist Mormonism as it could be without being lunar. Twin Oaks was founded in 1967 by flower children and devotees of behaviorist psychologist B.F. Skinner. The 100 people who composed my world were more likely to quote [communist philosopher] Karl Marx than [founder of the Mormon Church] Joseph Smith. The patriarchal structure of the FLDS [Fundamentalist Church of Jesus Christ of Latter-Day Saints] would have made every woman I knew at Twin Oaks scream for subversion. Twin Oaks' bylaws define the community as egalitarian. Its culture is decidedly feminist. When I was about 7, we had an all-female auto-maintenance crew. Yet like the FLDS children, I grew up in a place where my "normal" was far enough from the average American childhood to make *Dick and Jane* books read like cultural anthropology. Like the FLDS children, my caregivers were nearly innumerable. Sometimes, it seemed as if nobody in particular was raising us. The most striking similarity between my life and theirs is the sense of division you feel when you grow up somewhere that defines itself as an alternative to the dominant culture. The boundaries of the property become the boundaries of ideology, dividing right from wrong, us from them. I no longer read the division as a moral issue, but I still see a divide. That's why, particularly when the news is of "outsiders," I read the newscasters as closely as the news itself and remember my own childhood.

As a child, the grown-up I was closest to cooked my home-made mac and cheese (before the hippies learned to cook tofu in any edible form) and was the only one who could get me to take a bath. She had two long-term relationships during my childhood and had them simultaneously. Biologically speaking, she wasn't my mother—but saying so is emotionally false. When I woke up from a nightmare (in the room I shared with a girl who is not my sister, but there is no better term to describe the person with whom I shared a room for 10 years and on whom I attempted to blame most of my childhood's high crimes and misdemeanors), I would walk up two flights of stairs to be comforted by the purveyor of mac and cheese, warmth, and safety. On certain days of the week, there would be a black-haired man next to her; on other days, a blond. I knew these men tangentially, knew they were her lovers, and didn't give them much thought. Whichever man it was would shove over. I would crawl under the blankets. She would put an arm around me. I don't remember waking up there. She must have carried me back to bed after I fell asleep. The memory of moonlight is indelible.

Americans might have an extremely generous and expansive notion of alternative lifestyle choices. But our notions of what constitutes an acceptable childhood occupy a very narrow bandwidth.

Reconciling Two Different Cultures

Given the comfort of those memories, there's something in the voices of even the most tolerant newscasters covering the Texas story that bothers me. In a piece on the FLDS custody battle a couple of weeks ago, NPR's Howard Berkes reflected on the "amazing" polygamous women he has known—high-powered professionals who contrast with the image of bare-foot pregnant women inside a compound. Yet unease lurks even under their assertions that many strong, capable people are involved in polygamous marriage. That unease makes Berkes' protestations ring hollow as he refers to them as articulate. When the *New York Times* describes the teenage and 'tween-age girls getting ready to return home, the focus is on the "identical navy blue dresses they had sewn themselves." The *Times* quotes the director of a children's home as saying the clothes are "their way of celebrating." As she becomes the anthropologist introducing the reader to these "strange" girls, I wonder whether they're really so different from any other young ladies getting dressed up for a big event. Is the American imagination really so attenuated that we can't see excitement in these girls if they aren't on their way to prom?

The idea of 13-year-old girls being married to their uncles is indefensible.

Underneath the desire to embrace cultural relativism and alternative definitions of family lurks a deep inability to reconcile the children who were taken into state custody with America's picture of itself. Americans might have an extremely generous and expansive notion of alternative lifestyle choices. But our notions of what constitutes an acceptable childhood occupy a very narrow bandwidth. Given the hairline margin for deviation, it isn't really surprising that the state of Texas' desire to protect the FLDS children resulted in chaos.

I'm often asked what it was like to grow up "that way." Whoever I am talking with wants me to build a bridge connecting the strange and the familiar. I tell them I converted to Christianity for two months when I was 6 to irritate people. Two years later, that same motivation led me to ask to join the Girl Scouts, even though I knew they were considered a quasifascistic organization. (I still haven't figured out what the problem was there.) I try to give friends from the outside a sense of the summer when the community assigned someone to sit in a hammock and teach me—a dyslexic, headstrong little girl—to read. I also tell them about the hollow feeling that came when the adults I loved would wander off to find themselves. Many people return the favor by answering my questions about custody battles, church picnics, and the social function of betting on some phenomenon I am given to understand is referred to as "March Madness."

I don't have a huge polemic ax to grind where polygamy is concerned. The idea of 13-year-old girls being married to their uncles is indefensible. I'd call social services faster than you can say "alternative lifestyle" and happily pin the men in question to the wall until the cops showed up. Any of the members of nontraditional families I know would do the same, even while a month's worth of news causes them to worry that a phone call and a state decision could break apart their own families.

Looking Past Differences to Find Similarities

The next time an intentional community stands accused of crimes, whether it's of the FLDS, New Mexico's Strong City, or another group, social services must better understand these children's lives. The tacit recognition of strangeness seems to be a key feature of this story, but the willingness to see any sameness is absent. As soon as the specter of child abuses rises in the national consciousness, we seem to need to consider communities monstrous in every particular. Children will be removed with indecent haste and returned slowly. Still, I wonder what degree of empathy is possible in a social structure that persists in defining the lives of the children it is trying to help as bizarre.

I wonder whether the newscasters and social workers have a childhood memory like mine. They woke up in a house with one family and crawled into a bed whose occupants were conventionally associated with each other. It might be that they associate that feeling of comfort with the marriage that brought about that bed. I don't know. What I do know is that despite my own distance from that *Dick and Jane* family you know, and like the FLDS children returning home from what must be a frightening spring, I too remember a window full of moonlight, warm blankets, and an arm around me as I fell asleep.

8

Polygamy Should Be Legalized

Jeff Jared

Jeff Jared is an attorney specializing in family law and criminal defense and a contributor to the Kirkland Reporter. *He writes from a libertarian perspective on legal and economic issues.*

As long as polygamy is a marriage contract among consenting adults, it should be protected by Article I, Section 10 of the US Constitution, and states should not have the right to limit marriage to a union between one man and one woman. Criminalizing plural marriage violates freedom of religion and constitutes discrimination against a victimless lifestyle. As long as men and women enter polygamy of their own free will, and as long as their children do not suffer abuse, arguments against plural marriage are baseless.

Did you know that there are 40,000 underground polygamists in the U.S.? And a world religion, Islam, allows plural marriage, plus multiple spouses have been present in human cultures forever. So shouldn't polygamy be legal? Yes, because having multiple wives is a religious right and should be protected under the right to contract and/or substantive due process.

So what's wrong with multiple wives, especially if they're consenting adults? After all, consenting adults should be free to have group marriages, gay marriages, mail-order marriages, marriages for convenience, marriages for money, or any other

Jeff Jared, "Why Polygamy Should Be Legal," *Kirkland Reporter*, February 2010. www.kirklandreporter.com. Copyright © 2010 by Jeff Jared. All rights reserved. Reproduced by permission.

kind of marriage. This is just freedom of contract, a right found in Article I, Section 10 of the U.S. Constitution, which states that "No State shall enter into any . . . law impairing the obligation of contracts."

The Freedom of Contract Should be Protected

The right to contract for business is fundamental to the free enterprise system and so is the right to contract for social relationships like marriage. Family law in every state allows for social contracts in the marriage and family context. There are pre-nups, post-nups,[1] and separation agreements. The law encourages divorcing parties, and business parties, to freely contract to arrange and organize their affairs in a consensual fashion. Freedom of contract affirms the dignity and autonomy of the individual and is the mark of a legally and economically sophisticated society.

Alternative families take many forms and should be protected by law (up to and until there's a true victim). The state, in general, should be neutral on lifestyle and moral issues.

There's another reason to allow plural marriage: religious freedom. How dare the state or feds, or anybody else, tell worshipers how to practice their religion? Clearly if a fundamentalist sect threw virgins into volcanoes, the state could step in. But when there is no victim and thus no legitimate state interest, only consenting wives who'll tell you they're in of their own volition, then individual freedom should reign.

Criminalizing victimless sexual and intimate relations like this is misguided. I say "victimless," because criminalizing

---

1. Pre-nuptial (before marriage) and post-nuptial (after marriage) agreements are legal contracts regarding finances or other aspects of married life.

some private relations, like domestic violence—where there really is a victim—is acceptable. But laws regulating consensual relations between adults, like laws against polygamy, prostitution, sodomy, fellatio and the like, should be repealed.

Alternative lifestyles have always met with criticism. Opponents of early divorce laws thought they would legalize polygamy as people remarried. And cohabitation and having kids out of wedlock used to be spurned. All are now mainstream. Alternative families take many forms and should be protected by law (up to and until there's a true victim). The state, in general, should be neutral on lifestyle and moral issues.

Polygamy Has a Long History and Is Practiced in Many Places

"Bigamy" is the legal crime, under which people can be prosecuted for the act of marrying one woman while still married to another, while "polygamy" is having multiple wives. The modern term for more than one spouse is "plural marriage." "Polyandry" is having multiple husbands. Polygamy is more common in human cultures than polyandry.

Polygamy is legal in Muslim countries today, although fairly rare as the husband must be wealthy enough to support his wives. And polygamy was a tenet of the Mormon Church from 1840 until 1890 when the Church ended it because of federal threats to withhold statehood from Utah (achieved in 1896). Old Testament prophets took multiple wives and anthropologists will tell you that polygamy has been in human cultures throughout history.

Many accurately point out that some polygamist's wives are as young as 13 when they were married, which is illegal. (The age in Washington to marry without parental consent is 17.) But marrying at age 13 is legal in many states—with the consent of the parents—and is legal in some foreign countries. But whatever the age of consent is determined to be— and this is important because a marriage becomes statutory/

child rape if the girl is too young—plural and unorthodox marriages after this age should be legal.

It's often been said that "your rights stop at the tip of my nose." And similarly, the right to an alternative lifestyle stops at the age of consent. The right to contract is an adults-only right. Minors and mental incompetents don't qualify.

States Should Not Regulate Marriages

But outside of this, freedom of marriage should be the rule. Gay, polygamous and other alterative marriages should be legal private contracts, with or without the state. Absent coercion, duress, fraud, incapacity, insanity, underage, criminal conspiracy or other traditional common law contract defenses that can justify breaking contracts (or prevent enforcing such contracts), such alternative relationships should remain free of government regulation per substantive due process.

Once legal, polygamy would come out from the underground where it is harder to prosecute the real crimes that do occur in polygamous communities. With polygamy illegal, polygamists are reluctant to call police regarding real crimes like domestic violence, false imprisonment and rape.

And note that a human can't marry his pet because animals don't have rights and responsibilities under the constitution and American law wouldn't recognize such a marriage. You can set up a trust for your pet, but you can't marry it. Nor could you marry an inanimate object.

A man is not a criminal for having 5 wives. He may be bad for failing to pay the state back for welfare received, and he may be a legitimate criminal for marrying and having sex with an underage girl, or for rape, but absent that, the mere status of polygamy should not be a crime, but a protected right.

9

Canadian Judge Says Polygamy Ban Should Be Upheld

Jeremiah Hainsworth

Jeremiah Hainsworth is a contributor to AP Worldstream.

In the following viewpoint, a Canadian judge claims that a ban on polygamy should stay in place. Chief justice of British Columbia's highest court, Robert Bauman believes that the harm polygamy inflicts on women and children far outweighs any claims to religious freedom. The viewpoint argues that there is great harm found among polygamy, ranging from physical and sexual abuse to the subjugation of women. Harm is inherent in polygamy.

VANCOUVER, British Columbia (AP)—A Canadian judge ruled Wednesday that the country's anti-polygamy law is valid and that the harms polygamy inflicts on women and children outweigh any claims to religious freedom.

The chief justice of British Columbia's highest court, Robert Bauman, said in an individual ruling that banning the practice only minimally impairs the religious rights of fundamentalist polygamous Mormons.

Bauman accepted evidence that polygamy leads to harms including physical and sexual abuse, child brides, the subjugation of women and the expulsion of young men who have no women left to marry.

"This case is essentially about harm . . . to women, to children, to society and to the institution of monogamous marriage," wrote Bauman.

"There can be no alternative to the outright prohibition," he added. "There is no such thing as so-called 'good polygamy.'"

Upholding the law could lead to prosecutions in a small, polygamous community in British Columbia. George Macintosh, a lawyer appointed to oppose the anti-polygamy law at the hearings, said he would likely launch an appeal. The case is expected to wind up in Canada's Supreme Court.

FLDS members practice polygamy in arranged marriages, a tradition tied to the early theology of the Mormon church.

Prosecutors seeking clarity on the law brought the case after another judge threw out polygamy charges against Winston Blackmore and James Oler in 2009. Blackmore and Oler are rival bishops of the Fundamentalist Church of Jesus Christ of Latter Day Saints in Bountiful, a polygamous community of about 1,000 residents.

Blackmore has been accused of having at least 19 wives, and Oler at least 3.

FLDS members practice polygamy in arranged marriages, a tradition tied to the early theology of the Mormon church. The mainstream Church of Jesus Christ of Latter Day Saints renounced polygamy in 1890, but several fundamentalist groups seceded in order to continue the practice.

Blackmore has long claimed religious persecution and denial of a constitutional right to religious freedom. He said he would continue to fight.

"I certainly don't plan on dropping my faith and running away," he said. "The government has tried to do everything they could in the last 20 years to ruin our lifestyle. How can the Supreme Court of Canada uphold swinging and swapping clubs? A plural relationship doesn't kill anybody. The judge: he's wrong."

British Columbia Provincial Attorney General Shirley Bond declined to say when prosecutors could lay charges, particularly because of the likely appeals. She said the case was about polygamy's social harms.

"This case is about two competing visions—one of a personal harm versus state intrusion. As he clearly found, there is a profound harm associated with polygamy, particularly for women and children," Bond said.

Government lawyer Craig Jones said the judge found the harms of polygamy justified an infringement on personal freedom in the case.

Anne Wilde, a Mormon fundamentalist from Utah who testified at the hearings, said Utah's community will be generally disappointed by the decision. Wilde, co-founder of a plural culture advocacy group, is a widow who was one of three wives when her husband was alive.

"It's too bad that they have trouble separating the crime from the culture," said Wilde, who disagrees that there are harms inherent to polygamy. "There are already laws in place to address any criminal activity in any marriage lifestyle. Why don't they go ahead and enforce those laws rather than single out our culture?"

10

Polygamists Should Pay Higher Taxes, Not Be Criminalized

Economist

The Economist *is an English-language weekly news and international affairs publication, edited in London, England.*

Under current laws, legalizing polygamy would be a tax and welfare disaster, allowing multiple wives to receive health benefits, Social Security, and other federal and state support. Limiting marriage to two consenting adults is essential in our social system, but criminalizing polygamy is not the answer. Instead, people should be taxed according to the number of their spouses.

Sunday [July 24, 2011] marked the first day gay couples were allowed to marry in New York State. This provoked an unusual *New York Times* op-ed by lawyer Jonathan Turley. He reminds us of another group being robbed of their basic rights of citizenship—polygamists.

> The reason might be strategic: some view the effort to decriminalize polygamy as a threat to the recognition of same-sex marriages or gay rights generally. After all, many who opposed the decriminalization of homosexual relations used polygamy as the culmination of a parade of horribles. In his dissent in *Lawrence* [a landmark decision by the US Su-

preme Court in which the court struck down the sodomy law in Texas] Justice Antonin Scalia said the case would mean the legalization of "bigamy, same-sex marriage, adult incest, prostitution, masturbation, adultery, fornication, bestiality and obscenity."

Justice Scalia is right in one respect, though not intentionally. Homosexuals and polygamists do have a common interest: the right to be left alone as consenting adults. Otherwise he's dead wrong. There is no spectrum of private consensual relations—there is just a right of privacy that protects all people so long as they do not harm others.

Others have opposed polygamy on the grounds that . . . some polygamous families involve the abuse or domination of women. Of course, the government should prosecute abuse wherever it is found. But there is nothing uniquely abusive about consenting polygamous relationships. It is no more fair to prosecute [one polygamous family] because of abuse in other polygamous families than it would be to hold a conventional family liable for the hundreds of thousands of domestic violence cases each year in monogamous families.

Allowing Polygamy Would Be a Tax Disaster

Mr Turley claims he's not fighting for the state to recognise polygamous marriages, but he'd like to see the practice decriminalised. Though I am not quite sure what gay couples and polygamists have in common. The gay marriage cause is not about privacy. Rather, it's a quest to obtain equal rights, to ensure that gay spouses are protected, entitled to Social Security benefits, health insurance, and their partner's assets if the relationship ends through death or divorce. Extending these same rules to polygamy would be a fiscal nightmare. Could you imagine the expense of granting such privileges to someone with multiple spouses? Isn't Social Security already underfunded? Think of the cost to employers who must provide health insurance to one man and his seven wives. Imagine the litigation costs for a male breadwinner who dies unexpectedly without a will and with multiple dependent wives. Are assets divided evenly or based on how many children each wife produced? True, Mr Turley claims he's not asking for legal recognition of plural marriages, but his case does bring up some interesting economic questions.

For fiscal reasons alone, marriage should be limited to two consenting adults.

Economists often argue that polygamy (we'll focus on men marrying multiple women because that tends to be more common than polyandry, but the logic still applies to a woman with multiple husbands) benefits women because it enhances their market power. That's because it means more marriageable men for every woman. That may be true in the dating market, and as [economist] Gary Becker argues, probably explains why in polygamous cultures only wealthy men tend to have multiple wives. When a woman has more options, she will opt for a more productive and desirable spouse. Especially in an agrarian economy where a steady food supply is scarce, polygamy made sense, for men and women. Subsistence farming requires many children to provide free labour, so taking several wives was necessary. A woman would partake in the arrangement, because being part of a larger farm provided more safety, security, and resources for her and her children than being the only wife of a poor man.

Polygamy Puts Women at a Disadvantage

But once a woman enters into a polygamous arrangement, it seems she'd have less power. Bargaining power in a household is often based on who contributes what to household production and utility. Each person provides certain services and resources to make the household function and this keeps the marriage balanced. But the power structure is different when you have one man and several women. The marginal value each woman can uniquely provide diminishes the more women that are added to the family. In contrast, a male's services become relatively scarcer, so he will have more power within the marriage. That is, unless the wives manage to collude, though cartels tend to be inherently unstable.

You might argue that a woman retains some power because she can leave marriage and find someone else. After all, she has exceptional market power in the dating market. But terminating a marriage is costly, especially if the woman has children and is dependent on the man financially (and has no legal recognition). Also, in the sort of misogynistic cultures where polygamy thrives, a large premium is placed on a woman's ability to bear children. Under these circumstances her market value declines as she ages.

For fiscal reasons alone, marriage should be limited to two consenting adults. But the question of whether polygamy should be a criminal activity is a difficult one. It may not make sense for a modern woman to enter into such an arrangement, but bad judgment is not illegal. Also, lots of marriages have odd power dynamics; the state does not charge these couples with criminal activity. But polygamy may pose some negative externalities. It often leads to a large pool of unmarried, young men which can lead to social instability. And polygamists tend to have many children to support, which may prove to be a burden on the taxpayer. Rather than simply criminalising plural marriages, perhaps people should simply be taxed for each additional spouse.

11

Laws Against Polygamy Interfere with Civil Liberties

Wendy Kaminer

Wendy Kaminer, a lawyer and writer, has written several books on contemporary social issues, including A Fearful Freedom: Women's Flight From Equality, *about the conflict between egalitarian and protectionist feminism;* I'm Dysfunctional, You're Dysfunctional: The Recovery Movement and Other Self-Help Fashions; *and* Sleeping with Extra-Terrestrials: The Rise of Irrationalism and Perils of Piety.

It is unfair and a violation of civil liberties to deny fundamentalist Mormons the right to marry multiple wives and live according to the laws of their religion. Given that divorce and adultery have become common practice, society's outrage over plural marriage seems hypocritical. Furthermore, the notion that polygamy fosters child abuse and needs to be banned exposes a double-standard; after all, we have not outlawed alcohol even though it is seen as a contributing factor in sexual violence. Violence and child abuse are punishable offenses, and society should prosecute offenders instead of criminalizing marriages among consenting adults.

Opponents of gay rights often warn that legalizing same-sex marriage would inexorably lead to legalizing polygamy. Maybe it would, and maybe it should. Denying gay couples the right to marry violates state constitutional guarantees of equality, as the California and Massachusetts high courts have rightly ruled. (The Supreme Court of California also held that the right to marry is fundamental.) Surely Mormons have the same rights to equal treatment under law— and of course, they have a substantial First Amendment claim to engage in multiple marriages according to the dictates of their faith.

So why is polygamy illegal? Why don't Mormons have the right to enter into multiple marriages sanctified by their church, if not the state? There's a short answer to this question but not a very good one: polygamy is illegal and unprotected by the Constitution because the Supreme Court doesn't like it. Over one hundred years ago, the Court held in *Reynolds v. U.S.* that polygamy was "an offence against society." The *Reynolds* decision upheld the criminal conviction of a man accused of taking a second wife in the belief that he had a religious duty to practice polygamy, a duty he would violate at risk of damnation. The Court compared polygamy to murders sanctified by religious belief, such as human sacrifice or the burning of women on their husbands' funeral pyres.

Anti-Polygamy Laws Are Anachronistic

Even in Victorian America, this comparison made little sense. (Most Victorian women, I suspect, would have chosen polygamous marriages over death by burning.) Today the Court's analogy is as anachronistic as a ban on adultery. After all, what's the difference between an adulterer and a polygamist? And if it's not illegal for a married man to support a girlfriend or two and father children out of wedlock with them, how can it be illegal for him to bind himself to them according to the laws of his church? Why is a practicing Mormon with two wives a criminal while Staten Island Congressman Vito Fosella, recently embarrassed by the discovery of his second family, is simply a punchline? What's the moral and practical difference between a man who maintains multiple families without the approval of any church and a man who maintains multiple families with his church's approval?

Nontheists who favor civil unions for everyone—taking the state out of the business of approving or disapproving religious matrimonial rites—should be especially supportive of the First Amendment right to engage in polygamous marriages sanctified by any faith. Whether or not polygamy should be legalized so that people in polygamous marriages enjoy equal rights and entitlements (like Social Security benefits), it should at least be decriminalized. Why should we care about other people's private religious ceremonies? How dare we criminalize them?

We rightly prohibit violence, not drunkenness, even though some drunks are violent; we should prohibit child abuse, not polygamy, even though some polygamists are abusers.

Act Against Abuse, Do Not Outlaw Polygamy

"Polygamy encourages child abuse," people say, citing instances involving the marriage of older men to underage girls. Assuming for the sake of argument that this is true, it still doesn't justify categorical prohibitions on polygamy. Alcohol consumption may encourage sexual violence; it's often blamed for date rape. Should we prohibit its use, as members of the Women's Christian Temperance Union demanded over one hundred years ago? Or should we prosecute alcohol-fueled violence whenever we find it?

We rightly prohibit violence, not drunkenness, even though some drunks are violent; we should prohibit child abuse, not polygamy, even though some polygamists are abusers. To do otherwise is to court worse abuses than we seek to prevent, as the raid on the [Yearning] for Zion compound in Texas this past April [2008] demonstrated. On the basis of one anonymous phone call (that later appeared to be a hoax), Texas authorities forcibly removed more than 460 children from their parents without evidence of actual abuse in each case. Parents and children were ordered to undergo DNA testing (Who knows how long the state will maintain the DNA database, or to what uses it will be put?), and the children were summarily consigned to the notorious Texas foster-care system. They were subsequently reunited with their parents on order of Texas courts, which rightly held that the state had acted unlawfully, but who knows how much damage was done?

Some fools still compare homosexuality to bestiality, just as the Supreme Court once compared polygamy to human sacrifice.

It's hard to explain the relative complacency or cautiousness that initially greeted this extraordinary abuse of power, except with reference to religious bigotry or squeamishness about polygamy. Members of the [Yearning] for Zion sect tried taking their case to the public—some attorneys defended their rights, and the American Civil Liberties Union eventually expressed more than cautious concern for them—but predictably, the national conversation generally reflected little sympathy for the civil liberties of people involved in a religious group far outside the mainstream. Imagine the reaction had the state instead invaded a community of Christian Scientists and removed all their children after receiving an anonymous tip that one child had been harmed by the refusal of his or her parents to provide medical care.

States Should Not Abuse Their Power

The [Yearning] for Zion case is different, some reply, because polygamy is illegal. Exactly. Polygamy's illegality doesn't make the state's actions less abusive—imagine the reaction if the state summarily removed all the children from a commune in which parents were suspected of smoking dope—but it does provide authorities with an argument, however flawed.

Of course, I'm not suggesting that any parent have a religious right to harm their children by denying them medical care, subjecting them to sexual molestation, or otherwise abusing them. I'm simply pointing out that the state should not abuse the power to prosecute people or forcibly remove their children because authorities don't approve of their "lifestyle." Gay men were once routinely suspected of being pedophiles, a suspicion that persists today but with considerably less prevalence and respectability. Indeed, opposition to gay marriage still relies on specious arguments about the harm it poses to children. Some fools still compare homosexuality to bestiality, just as the Supreme Court once compared polygamy to human sacrifice. We progress when we base the extension of rights on reason, not bias or judicial hyperbole.

12

Polygamy Can Be a Viable Alternative Lifestyle

Christina Schimmel

Christina Schimmel is a writer, fashion blogger, and professional actress based in Toronto.

Committing adultery or dating several people at once is comparable to polygamy, and yet such practices are commonly accepted and carry little to no social stigma, though polygamy is reviled. Polygamists, despite their intentions of loving and caring for one another, must endure backlash from friends and family, and society ostracizes them. Widespread opposition to polygamy makes it difficult for people to enter into plural marriages, but those who choose to allow a third or fourth person to enter a relationship or marriage often find out that meaningful and loving bonds can be forged.

Just north of the city of Toronto, Lara lives on a farm with Tony, her common-law husband, and Lauren, the newest addition to their relationship [names have been changed for privacy reasons]. Lara is one of the many Canadians that has chosen the alternative lifestyle of polygamy. She has been open about her newer relationship status; publically announcing the decision on Facebook, declaring to her online public that she and Tony had now added a "sister wife", and that the three of them couldn't be happier.

Lara explains that living on a farm is tough work and likens the experience to the bygone years of the hunter-gatherer society from which we evolved; there is an extraordinary amount of work to be done with not enough people to complete it, and that having a polygamous family has solved these problems. This leads one to think about such "modern" ideas as farm hands that could have also sorted out these difficulties. Then, she of course sides with the anthropological view of monogamy that men always had to spread their seed, while women needed to have one man to take care of them, and all the other arguments that come with that standpoint.

Whenever someone has a husband or wife and also has another relationship on the side, [it] is in essence a form of polygamy.

Expanding the Family

Lauren has been staying on the farm since January of this year [2011], on a trial basis, and since everything has been going well she will be moving in permanently. Lara candidly explains that even though Tony and she have been together five years, in an on-and-off again, often tumultuous, relationship, she has inadvertently been in a polygamous relationship since the start. Unbeknownst to either woman, Tony had been dating both of them for the past five years.

Lara raises the fact about how many people actually do have polygamous relationships but are just dishonest about it, and don't label it as such, or are unaware like she had been. Whenever someone has a husband or wife and also has another relationship on the side, [it] is in essence a form of polygamy. They are engaging in two marriages essentially. She makes a great point of how much more common it actually is.

Earlier in their relationship, . . . Lara had learned of Tony's continuing trysts with the "other woman," prompting her to leave him. She loved him desperately, always returning to him. When they would get back together and things would seem fine, the ongoing relationship he had with Lauren continually resurfaced. Lara, like most romantic partners, wanted monogamy from her boyfriend.

Changing Views

Then came the breaking point; the topic of the three of them living together was re-introduced last fall and unlike in the beginning of Tony and Lara's relationship, she was starting to see things differently. After reflecting on a short relationship she had in the past with a polygamous man who had been open from the beginning about his ideals and watching the TLC reality show "Sister Wives", somehow her views had changed.

There have been difficulties in dealing with going public with the choice that she has made. She is estranged from her family in what she calls a "break", although Lauren and Tony's family are both accepting of their arrangement including his father who lives with them on the farm. The ongoing problems of wrestling with her jealousy and the added dynamics of a third person, with their wants and needs, is at times a lot to contend with.

Finding Acceptance

Lara does not endorse her way of life but wishes that people would be less judgmental and more accepting of her choice. Surprisingly, most people have been accepting. Their neighbors have been supportive as well as most friends. Of course there are some people that have not been understanding but Lara was expecting a far worse reaction than the one she has received. They currently do not have plans to expand their marriage with a third wife but at the same time she is not entirely against that idea either "if a woman came along who was the perfect fit". Whether you agree with her choices or not, to be so open about a taboo subject, one thing is certain, she is brave.

13

American Muslims Seek to Redefine Marriage

David J. Rusin

David J. Rusin is a research fellow at Islamist Watch. He has taken part in the Middle East Forum and has served as an editor at Pajamas Media for two years.

While polygamy might appear antiquated or sinful to some, Islam allows its practice, and therefore it is permissible for Muslim men to desire marrying multiple women. As the United States redefines its concept of marriage, some Muslims are trying to add the definition of polygamy. Islamists are using the argument for same-sex marriage as a comparison for polygamy. However, there are many opponents of polygamy, and Muslims will have a hard battle ahead of them to legalize it.

Presidential candidate Rick Santorum got jeered for comparing the legalization of same-sex marriage to that of polygamy, but, whether or not the comparison is rationally sound, thoughts of the former's facilitating the latter bring a smile to many Islamists. If the definition of marriage can evolve in terms of gender, some Muslims ask, why not in terms of number?

Islam sanctions polygamy—more specifically, polygyny—allowing Muslim men to keep up to four wives at once. Though marrying a second woman while remaining married to the first is prohibited across the Western world, including all 50 U.S. states, a Muslim can circumvent the law by wedding one woman in a government-recognized marriage and joining with others in unlicensed religious unions devoid of legal standing.

Accommodating a Growing Trend

As Muslims have grown more numerous in the West, so too have Muslim polygamists. France, home to the largest Islamic population in Western Europe, was estimated in 2006 to host 16,000 to 20,000 polygamous families—almost all Muslim—containing 180,000 total people, including children. In the United States, such Muslims may have already reached numerical parity with their fundamentalist-Mormon counterparts; as many as 100,000 Muslims reside in multi-wife families, and the phenomenon has gained particular traction among black Muslims.

The increasingly prominent profile of Islamic polygamy in the West has inspired a range of accommodations. Several governments now recognize plural marriages contracted lawfully in immigrants' countries of origin. In the United Kingdom [U.K.], these polygamous men are eligible to receive extra welfare benefits—an arrangement that some government ministers hope to kill—and a Scottish court once permitted a Muslim who had been cited for speeding to retain his driver's license because he had to commute between his wives.

The ultimate accommodation would involve placing polygamous and monogamous marriages on the same legal footing, but Islamists have been relatively quiet on this front, a silence that some attribute to satisfaction with the status quo or a desire to avoid drawing negative publicity. There have, of course, been exceptions. The Muslim Parliament of Great Britain made waves in 2000 about challenging the U.K.'s ban on polygamy, but little came of it. In addition, two of

Australia's most influential Islamic figures called for recognition of polygamous unions several years ago.

Redefining Marriage

With the legal definition of marriage expanding in various U.S. states, as it has in other nations, should we anticipate rising demands that we recognize polygamous marriages? Debra Majeed, an academic apologist for Islamic polygamy, has tried to downplay such concerns, claiming that "opponents of same-sex unions, rather than proponents of polygyny as practiced by Muslims, are the usual sources of arguments that a door open to one would encourage a more visible practice of the other." Yet some American Muslims apparently did not get the memo.

Because off-the-cuff remarks can be the most revealing, consider a tweet by Moein Khawaja, executive director of the Philadelphia branch of the radical Council on American-Islamic Relations (CAIR). After New York legalized same-sex marriage last June, Khawaja expressed what many Islamists must have been thinking: "Easy to support gay marriage today be it's mainstream. Lets see same people go to bat for polygamy, its the same argument. *crickets*"

Thirty-nine percent [of American Muslims] reported their intention to enter polygamous marriages if it becomes legal to do so.

The "same argument" theme is fleshed out in an October 2011 piece titled "Polygamy: Tis the Season?" in the *Muslim Link*, a newspaper serving the Washington and Baltimore areas. "There are murmurs among the polygamist community as the country moves toward the legalization of gay marriage," it explains. "As citizens of the United States, they argue, they should have the right to legally marry whoever they please, or however many they please." The story quotes several Muslim advocates of polygamy. "As far as legalization, I think they should," says Hassan Amin, a Baltimore imam who performs polygamous religious unions. "We should strive to have it legalized because Allah has already legalized it."

Again and again the article connects the normalization of same-sex marriage and Islamic polygamy. "As states move toward legalizing gay marriage, the criminalization of polygamy is a seemingly striking inconsistency in constitutional law," it asserts. "Be it gay marriage or polygamous marriage, the rights of the people should not be based on their popularity but rather on the constitutional laws that are meant to protect them."

Legalizing Polygamy

According to a survey carried out by the *Link*, polygamy suffers from no lack of popularity among American Muslims. Thirty-nine percent reported their intention to enter polygamous marriages if it becomes legal to do so, and "nearly 70 percent said they believe that the U.S. should legalize polygamy now that it is beginning to legalize gay marriage." Unfortunately, no details about the methodology or sample size are provided, and in general quality data on Western Muslims' views of polygamy are scarce and often contradictory. Results from a recent poll of SingleMuslim.com users, many of whom live in the West, show significant support for the religious institution of polygamy, while findings from a more professional-looking survey of French Muslims indicate little desire for legalization.

Nevertheless, the number of polygamous Muslims and the opportunity presented by the redefining of marriage make it very likely that direct appeals for official recognition will ramp up over the next decade, as more Muslims join vocal non-Muslims already laying out the case that polygamists deserve no fewer rights than gays. In the meantime, watch for Islamists and their allies to prepare for ideological battle.

For starters, one hears a lot about the alleged social necessity of recognizing Islamic polygamy. The hardships encountered by second, third, and fourth wives who lack legal protections are regularly highlighted, while polygamy is promoted as a solution to the loss of marriageable black men in America to drugs, violence, and prison. Because polygamists who are not legally married are known to abuse welfare systems—for instance, Muslim women in polygamous marriages often claim benefits as single mothers—it would not be shocking to see legalization pushed even as a means of curbing fraud.

These practical arguments are supplemented with heavy-handed attempts to extol the supposed virtues of Islamic polygamy, as in a Georgia middle-school assignment featuring a sharia-lauding Muslim who tells students that "if our marriage has problems, my husband can take another wife rather than divorce me, and I would still be cared for." Leftist academics such as Miriam Cooke, who has peddled the fiction that polygamy frees married Muslim women to pursue lovers, will have a role to play as well.

An Uphill Battle

The good news for opponents of polygamy is that eventual legalization remains far from certain in the U.S. or elsewhere. State representatives will not be rushing to introduce pro-polygamy bills when, according to a Gallup survey from last year, almost nine in ten Americans still see the practice as morally wrong. Opinions can change, of course, as they have regarding same-sex marriage. Unfortunately for polygamy's backers, however, the equality arguments employed to great effect by gay-marriage advocates may ring hollow, in that recognizing polygamy—which almost always takes the form of polygyny—would essentially endorse inequality between the genders.

Convincing American judges to overturn restrictions will be an uphill battle as well—and not just because of the U.S.

Supreme Court's 1879 rejection of the "religious duty" defense of marrying multiple partners in Reynolds v. United States. More recently, state supreme courts have explicitly held the line against polygamy in their rulings to extend marriage rights to same-sex pairs. See *Goodridge v. Department of Public Health* (Massachusetts, 2003) and *In re Marriage Cases* (California, 2008); the latter decision describes both polygamous and incestuous unions as "inimical to the mutually supportive and healthy family relationships promoted by the constitutional right to marry."

According to new research, Israeli Arab women in polygamous marriages are worse off than those in monogamous ones.

Judicial criticism of polygamy is not unique to the U.S. In a case concerning self-proclaimed Mormon fundamentalists, the supreme court of British Columbia upheld Canada's ban on plural marriage last November [2011] after the chief justice, in the words of the *New York Times*, "found that women in polygamous relationships faced higher rates of domestic, physical and sexual abuse, died younger and were more prone to mental illnesses. Children from those marriages, he said, were more likely to be abused and neglected, less likely to perform well at school and often suffered from emotional and behavioral problems."

Focusing on polygamy in the Islamic world does not yield a happier image. Based on her experiences in Afghanistan, feminist university professor Phyllis Chesler has called the practice "humiliating, cruel, [and] unfair to the wives," and noted that it "sets up fearful rivalries among the half-brothers of different mothers who have lifelong quarrels over their inheritances." Likewise, Egyptian-born human-rights activist Nonie Darwish has elucidated polygamy's "devastating impact on the healthy function and the structure of loyalties" within Muslim families.

Recent studies have bolstered these accounts. According to new research, Israeli Arab women in polygamous marriages are worse off than those in monogamous ones. A separate investigation uncovered similar negative effects on Malaysian Muslims. In addition, an academic paper released this year concludes that polygamous societies in general lag behind their monogamous counterparts and explores the reasons for this, including the increased tension and criminal activity that result from creating a surplus of single, low-status men.

There are many other arguments against polygamy that supporters of legalization will have to defeat, such as that expanding marriage to three or more people would require massive alterations of Western family law. However, neither bureaucratic obstacles nor public exposure of the social ills accompanying polygamy will deter polygamous Muslims from seeking what they desire.

Recognition of polygamous marriages would be a major win for stealth jihadists—and the time is nearly optimal for them to make their move. How ironic that laws benefiting gay couples may aid Islamists—followers of an ideology that despises homosexuals—in their campaign to establish sharia [Islamic law] in the Western world.

14

American Muslims Should Not Practice Polygamy

Engy Abdelkader

Engy Abdelkader is a legal fellow with the Institute for Social Policy and Understanding and a human rights attorney based in the New York/New Jersey area. In February 2009, her immigration work with survivors of torture fleeing persecution from all parts of the world was recognized with an award from the International Institute of New Jersey. Abdelkader is co-founder and the first president of the New Jersey Muslim Lawyers Association (NJMLA).

Within the Muslim world, views on polygamy—and interpretations of Islamic law regarding that practice—vary widely. Some liberal Islamic scholars say the Quran implicitly prohibits polygamy; more conservative scholars assert that it is permitted but discouraged. Regardless of such interpretations, Islamic law dictates that Muslims have to abide by the laws of the countries they inhabit. Because the United States prohibits polygamy, American Muslims cannot legally engage in the practice.

About a week or so ago [October 2011], I was invited to participate in a town hall focusing on religious freedom in America and the contagion of so-called "anti-Sharia" legislation [Sharia law is the moral code and religious law of Islam] around the country, when the topic of Muslim sister wives arose.

By way of background, approximately 50 "anti-Sharia" bills have been introduced in more than 20 states and three have passed, including those in Oklahoma, Louisiana and Tennessee. The "Save Our State Amendment"—the constitutional state amendment of which about 70 percent of Oklahoma voters approved last November—forbade courts from even "considering" Sharia and it was subsequently enjoined by a federal district Judge prior to certification by the state Board of Elections.

The Judge did so on the grounds that it is most likely unconstitutional as it would infringe upon the peaceful practice of religion by American Muslims guaranteed by the First Amendment of the U.S. Constitution.

It always amuses me that men who may know little else about the Islamic faith seem to know about the ostensible right to four wives.

I was specifically asked to address the civil rights implications of such legislation for the American Muslim community. It is worth noting that observance of Sharia is typically a private and personal matter for observant Muslims. For instance, volunteering at a soup kitchen or donating money to the local food bank is observance of Sharia. Showing kindness to animals is observance of Sharia. Refraining from lying, backstabbing, cheating or stealing is observance of Sharia. Compassion, mercy and forgiveness towards others is observance of Sharia.

What about polygamy?

As with most town halls, a robust Q and A ensued and I was asked about the Islamic practice of polygamy within the American Muslim community. The topic—shrouded in misunderstanding—necessitates brief discussion and clarification.

The Muslim world is frequently regarded as misogynistic and the misplaced belief that Muslim men may unconditionally marry up to four wives may contribute to the stereotype. (It always amuses me that men who may know little else about the Islamic faith seem to know about the ostensible right to four wives.)

Differing Views on Polygamy

To be sure, there are liberal and conservative interpretations of the Quranic verses pertaining to polygamy within Islamic Law.

According to liberal interpretations, polygamy is a pre-Islamic practice and Islamic Law attempted to limit it by restricting the number of wives permitted. Polygamy was not only practiced without restriction by the pagan Arabs who inhabited the Arabian peninsula at the time, but also by adherents in other faith communities as well. In fact, polygamy continues to be practiced in other faith communities today and has inspired shows like "Big Love" on HBO.

Some liberal Islamic scholars go so far as to say that the Quran implicitly prohibits polygamy. Proponents of this liberal viewpoint argue: while polygamy is permitted, the very Quranic verse sanctioning the practice also prescribes a condition to its exercise, a condition which God Himself admits is exceedingly difficult to fulfill which is treating co-wives with perfect equality.

These scholars point to the verse in the Quran which states, "You are never able to be fair and just as between women, even if it is your ardent desire" [Chapter 4, verse 29]. They claim that the conditions attached to polygamy are so rigorous as to make it a practical impossibility.

The conservative viewpoint on the subject is that polygamy is permitted but frowned upon.

These more conservative scholars argue that the Quranic verse regarding polygamy was revealed in the immediate aftermath of a battle some 1500 years ago against pagan Arabs where a large number of Muslim men were killed and a lot of women and children were left unprotected in what was largely a tribal society.

In contrast, polygamy is habitually misunderstood by some proponents in the context of satiating men's sexual appetite. Yet, this is largely attributable to cultural bias without sound basis in Islamic doctrine.

The Laws of the Land

What about the American Muslim community?

Islamic Law requires adherents to abide by the laws of the land in which they reside. Regardless of whether an American Muslim subscribes to a liberal or conservative viewpoint of polygamy, as noted above, they are religiously prohibited from engaging in polygamous relationships because it is illegal in the United States to do so.

End of inquiry.

Organizations to Contact

The editors have compiled the following list of organizations concerned with the issues debated in this book. The descriptions are derived from materials provided by the organizations. All have publications or information available for interested readers. The list was compiled on the date of publication of the present volume; names, addresses, phone and fax numbers, and e-mail and Internet addresses may change. Be aware that many organizations take several weeks or longer to respond to inquiries, so allow as much time as possible.

Americans Against Abuses of Polygamy (AAAP)
e-mail: info@polygamyisabuse.org
website: http://polygamyisabuse.com

Americans Against Abuses of Polygamy is a nonprofit, conservative feminist, human rights organization, based in Texas. The AAAP wants to educate the public on the human rights abuses found within the cultural practice of polygamy, worldwide and in the United States, and the potential dangers of decriminalization. The website offers articles on polygamy, as well as books about the negative aspects of the practice.

Amnesty International
5 Penn Plaza, New York, NY   10001
(212) 807-8400 • fax: (212) 627-1451
e-mail: aimember@aiusa.org
website: www.amnestyusa.org

Amnesty International is a global movement of people fighting injustice and promoting human rights. The organization works to protect people wherever justice, freedom, truth, and dignity are denied. Amnesty International investigates and exposes abuses, educates the public, and seeks to help transform societies to create a safer, more just world. Its website provides news and reports from around the world, including several examinations of human rights abuses associated with polygamy.

Campaign Against Polygamy and Women Oppression International (CAPWOI)

PO Box 54, Manchester   M40 8YZ
  United Kingdom
+44 (870) 160-3844
e-mail: capwoi@polygamystop.org
website: www.polygamystop.org

The Campaign Against Polygamy and Women Oppression International consists of women and men creating global awareness for the less publicized dangers of polygamy for women and children. CAPWOI campaigns against polygamy because the organization believes the practice breeds oppression, corruption, poverty, sexual immorality, overpopulation, mass illiteracy, and the spread of pandemic diseases. Its goal is a total ban on polygamy in Africa, the Middle East, and most parts of the Third World. CAPWOI provides news online and also sells books, such as *Polygamists' Wives*, to educate the public.

Child Protection Project
website: www.childpro.org

The Child Protection Project is dedicated to raising awareness about issues of child abuse within religiously affiliated polygamous communities and other religious organizations. The organization is particularly focused on how institutions, especially churches, ignore child abuse reporting requirements, and thus cause unnecessary suffering and pain to children and families. Articles and reports are made available on its website, as well as links to like-minded organizations for further research.

Christian Polygamy
website: www.christianpolygamy.com

This pro-polygamy website offers advice to men and women in polygamous relationships and to those interested in the practice. Books such as *Prince of Sumba, Husband to Many Wives* and *A Dialog on Polygamy* can be purchased online.

The HOPE Organization

115 N 300 W Bldg. B, Suite 101, Washington, UT   84780
(435) 627-9582
e-mail: the_hope_org@yahoo.com
website: www.thehopeorg.org

The HOPE Organization, a partner of the United Way, is a nonprofit group whose objective is to assist people making the transition from a polygamous lifestyle to mainstream society, empowering women and children to gain confidence and set their lives on track. The intent of the organization is to expose the abuses that take place within polygamist groups—not to abolish the practice. The organization's website includes a database of information pertaining to the topic, featuring countless articles from the *Salt Lake Tribune, Washington Post,* and other local and national media.

Principle Voices

e-mail: admin@principlevoices.org
website: www.principlevoices.org

Principle Voices is a nonprofit advocacy organization working on behalf of polygamous families to educate others about polygamous culture, to encourage empowerment of individuals and families from polygamous communities, and to provide crisis referrals and response to those in the culture. Its extensive website offers book reviews, essays, papers, and reading lists, as well as legal opinions.

Bibliography

Books

Claire Avery   *Hidden Wives*. New York: Forge
Books, 2010.

Sanjiv   *Secrets and Wives: The Hidden World*
Bhattacharya *of Mormon Polygamy*. Berkeley, CA:
Soft Skull Press, 2011.

Sam Brower   *Prophet's Prey: My Seven-Year
Investigation into Warren Jeffs and the
Fundamentalist Church of Latter-Day
Saints*. New York: Bloomsbury, 2011.

Joe Darger, Alina *Love Times Three: Our True Story of a
Darger, Vicki   Polygamous Marriage*. New York:
Darger, and   HarperOne, 2011.
Valerie Darger

Andrew   *Polygamy*. MI: Pieta Publishing, 2011.
Gurlowski

Brian Hales   *Modern Polygamy and Mormon
Fundamentalism: The Generations
After the Manifesto*. Draper, UT: Greg
Kofford Books, 2007.

Cardell Jacobson *Modern Polygamy in the United
and Lara Burton States: Historical, Cultural, and Legal
Issues*. New York: Oxford University
Press, 2011.

Brent Jeffs and *Lost Boy*. New York: Broadway Books,
Maia Szalavitz 2009.

Carolyn Jessop *Escape*. New York: Broadway Books,
and Laura Palmer 2007.

Carolyn Jessop and Laura Palmer
Triumph: Life After the Cult: A Survivor's Lessons. New York: Random House, 2010.

Miriam Koktvedgaard Zeitzen
Polygamy: A Cross-Cultural Analysis. London, United Kingdom: Berg, 2008.

John Llewellyn
Polygamy's Rape of Rachael Strong: Protected Environment for Predators. Scottsdale, AZ: Agreka Books, 2006.

Brian Mackert and Susan Martins Miller
Illegitimate: How a Loving God Rescued a Son of Polygamy. Colorado Springs, CO: David C. Cook, 2008.

Keith McMahon
Polygamy and Sublime Passion: Sexuality in China on the Verge of Modernity. Honolulu, HI: University of Hawaii Press, 2010.

Ron du Preez, ed.
Pathology of Polygamy: Cross-Cultural Mission on a Biblical Basis. Berrien Springs, MI: Omega Media, 2007.

James Sanbourne
My Mormon Life: A Boy's Struggle with Polygamy, Magic Underwear, and Racism. Seattle, WA: CreateSpace, 2011.

Walter Scheidel
Sex and Empire: A Darwinian Perspective. Palo Alto, CA: Stanford University, 2006.

Susan Ray Schmidt
Favorite Wife: Escape from Polygamy. Guilford, CT: Lyons Press, 2009.

Stephen Singular — *When Men Become Gods: Mormon Polygamist Warren Jeffs, His Cult of Fear, and the Women Who Fought Back*. New York: St. Martin's Press, 2008.

Irene Spencer — *Cult Insanity: A Memoir of Polygamy, Prophets, and Blood Atonement*. New York: Center Street, 2009.

Kim Taylor — *Daughters Of Zion: A Family's Conversion to Polygamy*. Grants Pass, OR: Rogue Hill Publishing, 2008.

Elissa Wall and Lisa Pulitzer — *Stolen Innocence*. New York: William Morrow, 2008.

Debra Weyermann — *Answer Them Nothing: Bringing Down the Polygamous Empire of Warren Jeffs*. Chicago, IL: Chicago Review Press, 2011.

Ann Eliza Young — *Wife No. 19: The Life and Ordeals of a Mormon Woman During the 19th Century*. Carlisle, MA: Applewood Books, 2009.

Periodicals and Internet Sources

Divya A — "Bigamy: An Issue of One Too Many," *Times of India*, September 13, 2009.

Brooke Adams and Mark Havnes — "Utah, Arizona Law Officers Descend Upon Polygamous Community," *Salt Lake City Tribune*, April 6, 2010.

Susan Frelich Appleton — "Parents by the Numbers," *Hofstra Law Review*, 2008.

Associated Press   "Polygamous Church Dispute May Head to Utah Court," May 1, 2011. www.ap.org.

BBC News   "Nigerian Faces Death for 86 Wives," BBC News, August 21, 2008.

Daphne Bramham   "Polygamy, Impunity and Human Rights," *Inroads*, Summer 2008.

Thom Brooks   "The Problem with Polygamy," *Philosophical Topics*, 2009.

Bob Chodos   "The Religious Test," *Inroads*, Winter 2009.

Susan G. Cole   "Pick Your Poison," *Herizons*, Winter 2011.

Chuck Colson and Timothy George   "The 'Big Love' Strategy: What Are Americans Learning from Pop Culture Portrayals of Polygamy?" *Christianity Today*, October 18, 2011. www.christianitytoday.com.

Akua Djanie   "The Sins of Our Fathers," *New African*, July 2009.

Jennifer Dobner   "Polygamous Church in Utah Names New President," Associated Press, February 15, 2010. www.ap.org.

Catherine Elsworth   "My Family and Other Animals: My Life as the Wife of a Polygamist," *Telegraph* (United Kingdom), September 23, 2007.

Jaime Gher   "Polygamy and Same-Sex Marriage—Allies or Adversaries Within the Same-Sex Marriage Movement," *William & Mary Journal of Women & the Law*, 2008.

Hilary Hylton   "A New Prophet for the Polygamists?" *Time*, July 18, 2008.

Antonina Kerner   "Polygamous Family to Challenge Utah's Bigamy Law," *Human Events*, July 18, 2011.

Charles Kindregan Jr.   "Religion, Polygamy, and Non-Traditional Families: Disparate Views on the Evolution of Marriage in History and in the Debate over Same-Sex Unions," *Suffolk University Law Review*, 2007.

New York Times   "Texas: Polygamist Leader Convicted," August 4, 2011. www.nytimes.com.

Jared Rosenberg   "Polygynous Marriage Linked to Higher Child Mortality," *International Perspectives on Sexual and Reproductive Health*, 2009.

Luiza Ch. Savage   "On Polygamy, Child Brides and Why the Stakes in B.C. Are So High: Carolyn Jessop in Conversation with Luiza Ch. Savage," *Maclean's*, April 4, 2011. www2.macleans.ca.

Mark Strasser   "Marriage, Free Exercise, and the Constitution," *Law & Inequality*, 2008.

Joe Treasure   "Polygamy: Wives and Republicans," *New Statesman*, September 24, 2007.

Matthew Waller   "FLDS Member Found Guilty of Child Sexual Assault," *San Angelo Standard-Times*, June 22, 2010.

Washington Times   "Anti-Polygamy Law Challenged in Canada Court," January 5, 2011.

Washington Times   "Same-Sex Marriages Give Polygamy a Legal Boost," March 21, 2011.

Lindsey Whitehurst   "'Sister Wives' Polygamy Lawsuit Tackles Privacy in Utah," *Salt Lake Tribune*, July 13, 2011.

Index